CAROL VORDERMAN
Maths Made Easy

10
Minutes
A Day

Maths

Ages
5-7

DK

Author Deborah Lock
Consultant Sean McArdle

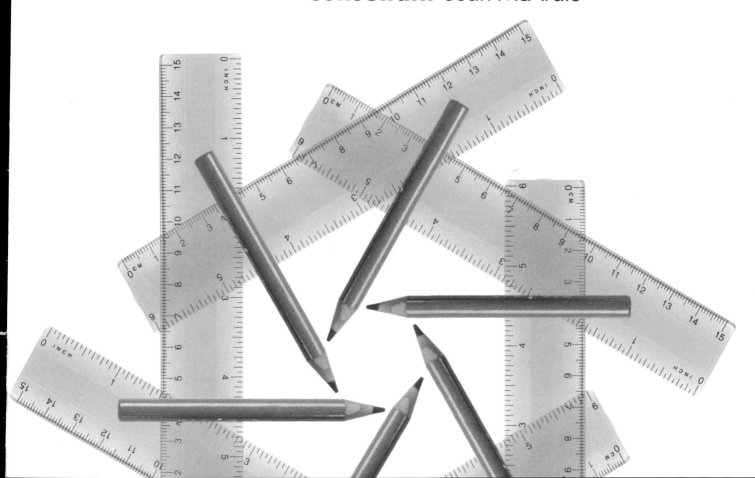

T0368800

10-minute challenge

Try to complete the exercises for each topic in 10 minutes or less. Note the time it takes you in the "Time taken" column below.

DK London
Editor Elizabeth Blakemore
Senior Editor Deborah Lock
Managing Editor Christine Stroyan
Managing Art Editor Anna Hall
Maths Consultant Sean McArdle
Senior Production Editor Andy Hilliard
Senior Production Controller Jude Crozier
Jacket Design Development Manager Sophia MTT
Publisher Andrew Macintyre
Associate Publishing Director Liz Wheeler
Art Director Karen Self
Publishing Director Jonathan Metcalf

DK Delhi
Senior Editor Rupa Rao
Designers Priyabrata Roy Chowdhury, Anuj Sharma, Aanchal Singal, Priyanka Singh
Managing Editors Soma B. Chowdhury, Kingshuk Ghoshal
Managing Art Editor Govind Mittal
DTP Designers Anita Yadav, Rakesh Kumar, Harish Aggarwal
Senior Jacket Designer Suhita Dharamjit
Jackets Editorial Coordinator Priyanka Sharma

This edition published in 2020
First published in Great Britain in 2013 by
Dorling Kindersley Limited
20 Vauxhall Bridge Road,
London SW1V 2SA

The authorised representative in the EEA is
Dorling Kindersley Verlag GmbH. Arnulfstr. 124,
80636 Munich, Germany

Copyright © 2013, 2020 Dorling Kindersley Limited
A Penguin Random House Company
25 24 23 22 21
023–186126–Apr/2020

A CIP catalogue record for this book
is available from the British Library.
ISBN: 978-1-4093-6541-9

Printed and bound in the UK

All images © Dorling Kindersley Limited

www.dk.com

This book was made with Forest Stewardship Council™ certified paper – one small step in DK's commitment to a sustainable future.
Learn more at www.dk.com/uk/information/sustainability

Contents

Time taken

Place value

The position of the digits 0–9 in a number gives its value. Start the timer!

1 Write 26 in words.

....

2 What number is this?

Hundred	Ten	Unit

3 Write these numbers as digits.

Twelve

Forty nine

Seventy two

4 What is the largest number you can make with the digits 3, 5, and 8?

(5) Draw the pictures
for these numbers.
Use these blocks.

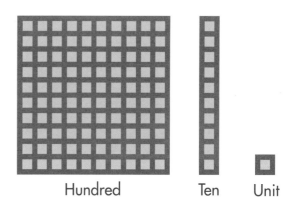

Hundred   Ten   Unit

9	37

254

Measuring length

These questions are all about length.
You will need a ruler. Start the timer.

① Which is longer? Tick (✔) the answer.

☐ A car

☐ A bus

② What would you use to measure your height?
Tick (✔) the answer.

☐ Measuring tape

☐ Weighing scales

③ Match the object with its length. Draw a line.

2 metres

345 metres

20 centimetres

Time filler:
Remember: 1 cm = 10 mm, 1 m =100 cm, and 1 km = 1,000 m. Try changing 5 cm into mm (millimetres), 5 m into cm (centimetres), and 5 km into m (metres). Write your own conversion problems like this.

④ How long are these lines in centimetres (cm)? Use a ruler.

⑤ Jake walked 2 km to the shops and then walked 2 km back the same way. How far had he walked altogether?

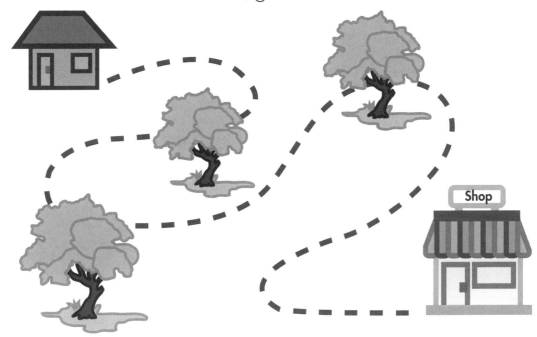

Counting

You will need a die for question 4.
When you are ready, start the timer.

(1) Fill in the gaps.

11   12   13   ☐   ☐   ☐   17   ☐   19   ☐

(2)   Which tree has the most apples? Tick (✔) the answer.

(3) How many biscuits are there on the baking tray?

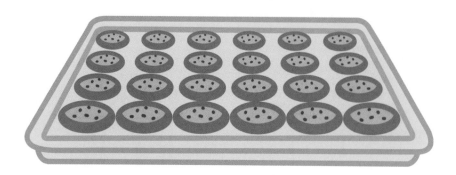

Time filler:
Count how many t-shirts you have in your drawers. Count how many plates are in the cupboard and how many mugs are in the kitchen.

4) Use a die. Start at 0. Roll the die and count on the number shown until you reach the end. Circle the numbers you land on.

0	1	2	3	4	5	6	7	8	9	10	11
											12

24	23	22	21	20	19	18	17	16	15	14	13
25											

26	27	28	29	30	31	32	33	34	35	36	37
											38

50	49	48	47	46	45	44	43	42	41	40	39

5) Riley put 6 red pens into a jar and then put 7 blue pens in the same jar. How many pens are there in the jar? Use the number line to help you count.

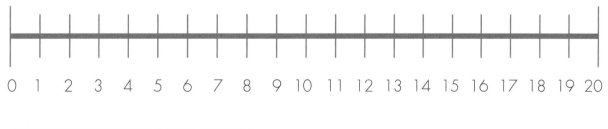

0 1 2 3 4 5 6 7 8 9 10 11 12 13 14 15 16 17 18 19 20

2-D shapes

A two-dimensional shape is a flat shape. Are you ready to test your knowledge? You will need a ruler.

(1) Which shape is a circle? Tick (✔) the answer.

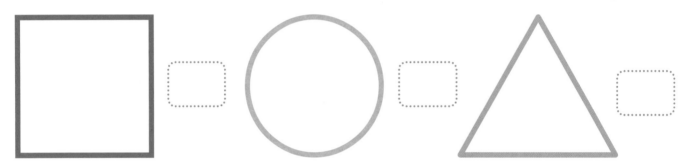

(2) How many sides does a rectangle have?

(3) Match the shape to its name. Draw a line.

Octagon

Hexagon

Square

Time filler:
Remember: A regular shape has all sides and angles that are equal. Can you find any regular shapes in your home? Are the windows regular? Is it easier to find regular or irregular shapes?

④ Which shape is regular? Tick (✔) the answer.

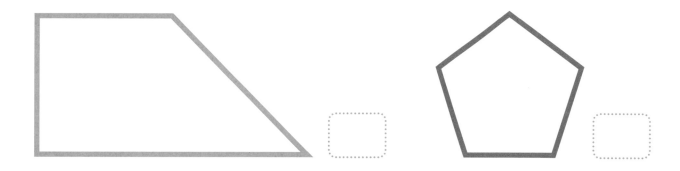

⑤ Use a ruler. Draw a triangle.

12

Counting in leaps

Try counting in 2s, 5s, and 10s.
Get set, go!

(1) Count in 2s. Fill in the gaps.

2 ☐ 6 ☐ 10 ☐ ☐ 16 ☐ 20

(2) Here is a number line. Start at 7 and show the leaps to add 2 more each time.

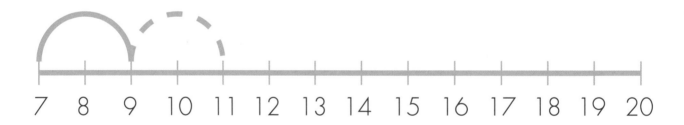

7 8 9 10 11 12 13 14 15 16 17 18 19 20

(3) Work out the missing numbers.

12 22 32 ☐ ☐ 62 ☐

5 10 ☐ 20 ☐ ☐ 35 ☐

24 22 ☐ 18 ☐ 14 ☐ 10

(4) What is 5 more than 45?

(5) This machine adds 10 to numbers. Add 10 to the numbers going IN and write the answers coming OUT.

OUT

IN

3 →
6 →
8 →
12 →
35 →

+ 10

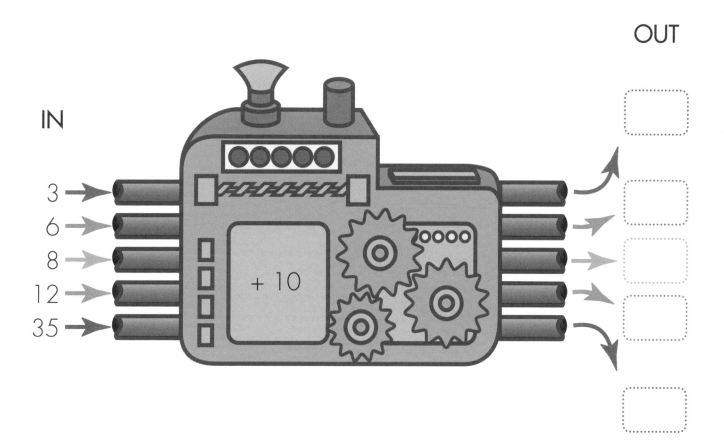

Tables and charts

Showing information on tables and charts is a useful way of reading and comparing that information. Start the clock and have a go!

A class of 20 children were asked to vote for their favourite wild animal. The results were shown on this table.

Wild animal	Number of children
Elephant	4
Lion	5
Monkey	3
Hippo	2
Tiger	4
Giraffe	2

1) Which was the most popular wild animal?

....

2) How many children voted for the monkey?

3) Which animals had the least votes?

....

Time filler:
Ask your family and friends to vote for their favourite wild animal. Choose either a table or chart to show the number of votes for each animal.

(4) Look at the table and colour the correct number of squares on the chart below.

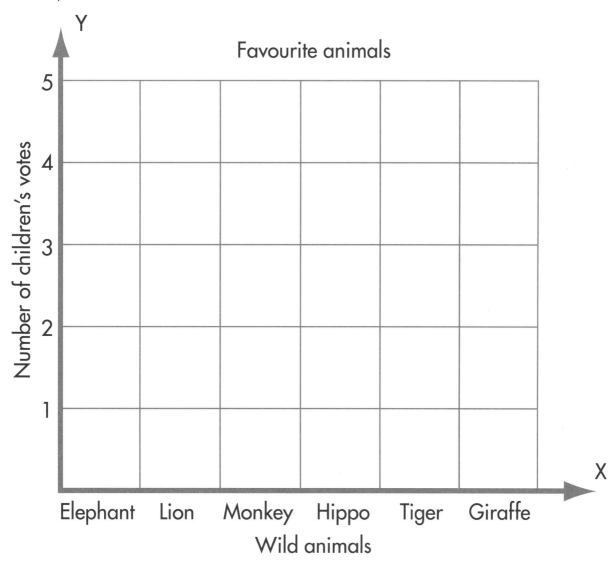

(5) Looking at the chart, how many more children voted for the elephant than the hippo?

Number order

Here is some number fun!
Put them in the correct order.

(1) Put these numbers in the correct order. Start from the smallest.

36   75   24   9   52

☐   ☐   ☐   ☐   ☐

(2) What comes next?

56   57   58   ☐   ☐   ☐

27   32   37   ☐   ☐   ☐

63   66   69   ☐   ☐   ☐

(3) Circle the largest number.

26   19   37   31

Time filler:
How many numbers can you make using one or more of the digits 4, 8, and 2? Write them down and then write them again in order. Start with the smallest.

(4) Put these numbers in the correct order. Start from the biggest.

67   42   53   48   59

(5) Which number is halfway between 16 and 24?
Use the number line to help.

15   16   17   18   19   20   21   22   23   24   25

Lines of symmetry

A shape that can be folded exactly
in half is called symmetrical.
The fold is a line of symmetry.

1 Draw one line of symmetry on these shapes.

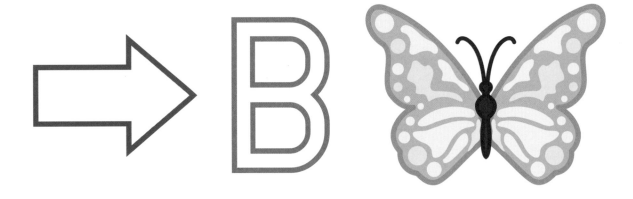

2 How many lines of symmetry does the letter H have?

3 Draw lines of symmetry on this regular
pentagon. How many lines are there?

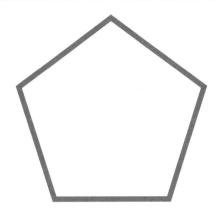

Time filler:
Can you find 10 things around your home that have one or more lines of symmetry?

4) Circle the shape that is not symmetrical.

5) Complete the picture by drawing the other half.
Colour the pattern so that it is symmetrical.

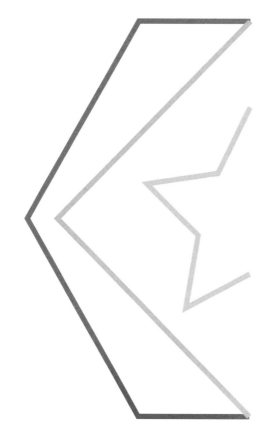

Beat the clock 1

Write these numbers as digits.
How many can you do in 10
minutes? Start the clock.

1 Nine

2 Twelve

3 Twenty two

4 Sixteen

5 Three

6 Thirty two

7 Eight

8 Four

9 Eleven

10 One

11 Twenty seven

12 Thirty eight

13 Forty three

14 Eighteen

15 Seven

16 Fifty six

17 Thirty three

18 Fourteen

19 Twenty one

20 Fifteen

21 Forty

22 Sixty nine

23 Eighty

24 Fifty three

25 Twenty

26 Forty five

27 Fifty one

28 Nineteen

29 Five

30 Sixty four

Time filler:
Have you checked your answers? Then stop the timer. How long did it take you? Mark the answers. They are on page 80.

31 Eighty seven

32 Thirty

33 Forty four

34 Eighty two

35 Sixty one

36 Forty nine

37 Twenty six

38 Fifty five

39 Ten

40 Seventy seven

41 Thirteen

42 Sixty six

43 Ninety eight

44 Seventy three

45 Thirty four

46 Eighty one

47 One hundred

48 Twenty five

49 Sixty

50 Ninety five

51 Seventy six

52 Eighty four

53 Thirty seven

54 Seventy five

55 Eighty eight

56 Ninety two

57 Fifty seven

58 Forty eight

59 Sixty two

60 Ninety nine

Adding numbers

Total, sum, and altogether all mean
to add together the numbers given.
Give it a go!

① What is the total of 5 and 8?

② Add together 12 and 16.

③ Fill out these steps:

40 + 20 =

8 + 6 =

48 + 26 =

(4) Complete these sums:

$$
\begin{array}{r} 28 \\ + 11 \\ \hline \end{array}
\qquad
\begin{array}{r} 34 \\ + 25 \\ \hline \end{array}
\qquad
\begin{array}{r} 52 \\ + 37 \\ \hline \end{array}
\qquad
\begin{array}{r} 47 \\ + 19 \\ \hline \end{array}
$$

(5) 32 children went to school in one bus and 27 children in another bus. How many children were there altogether?

Measuring weight

These questions are all about weight. Start the timer.

① Which is heavier? Tick (✔) the answer.

☐ An elephant

☐ A dog

② What would you use to weigh some sugar?
Circle the answer.

A measuring jug

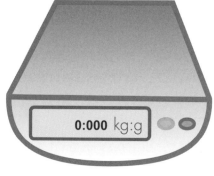

Weighing scales

③ Match the object with its weight. Draw a line.

 An apple   1 kilogram

 A bag of sugar   1 tonne

 A small car   100 grams

Time filler:
With an adult, choose a recipe
to bake. Help to weigh out the
ingredients you will need.

④ Look at these scales. How much do these bags weigh?

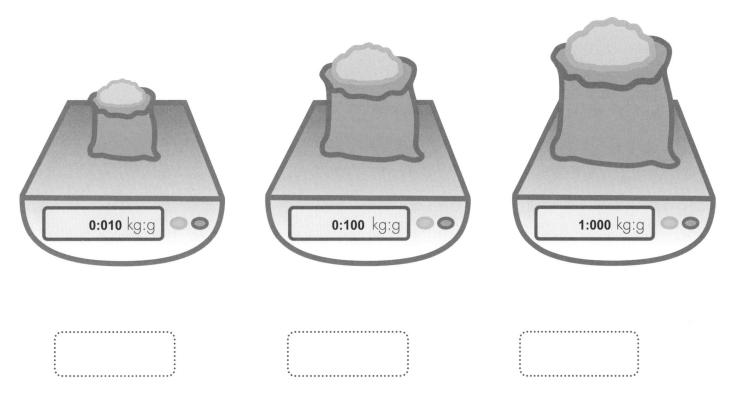

0:010 kg:g

0:100 kg:g

1:000 kg:g

⑤ Kia measured 50 grams of butter into a mixing bowl and
then added 25 grams of sugar. What was the total weight?

Subtracting numbers

Difference, take away, and less than all mean to subtract the numbers given. Start the timer!

1. What is the difference between 18 and 5?

2. Take away 26 from 58.

3. Fill out these steps.

30 − 28 =

64 − 30 =

64 − 28 =

Time filler:
Make two numbers with one or more of the digits 3, 2, and 4, such as 42. Now subtract the two numbers. Make some more numbers by using the digits more than once, such as 22. Subtract these new numbers.

4 Complete these questions.

25	38	55	47
− 13	− 24	− 37	− 19

5 Anya had a bag of 50 sweets. She gave 28 sweets to her friends. How many did she have left?

3-D shapes

A three-dimensional shape is a solid shape. Are you ready to test your knowledge? Go!

① Which shape is a cube? Tick (✔) the answer.

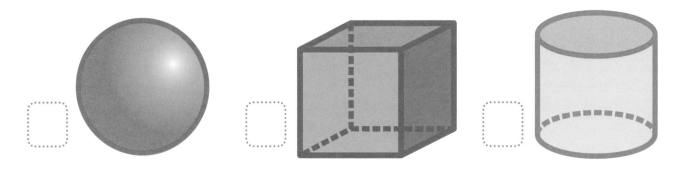

② How many faces does a square-based pyramid have?

③ Match the shape to its name. Draw a line.

Triangular prism

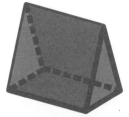

Cuboid

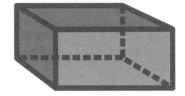

Cone

Time filler:
Look around your home. Make a list
of objects that are a sphere shape, a
cuboid shape, or a cylinder shape.
What other 3-D shapes can you find?

(4) How many edges do these shapes have?

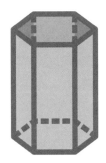

Hexagonal prism

Triangle-based
pyramid

Sphere

(5) Which shape has the most vertices (corners)?
Circle the answer.

Sequences

Can you spot the number sequences? They can go either up or down.

(1) Fill in the missing numbers.

6   10   14   [ ]   22   [ ]   [ ]

23   30   37   [ ]   [ ]   58   [ ]

(2) Circle the odd numbers in this sequence.

4   7   10   13   16   19

(3) Fill in the missing numbers.

44   42   [ ]   [ ]   [ ]   34   [ ]

73   70   67   [ ]   [ ]   58   [ ]

Time filler:
Can you count up in even numbers from 2? Can you count up in odd numbers from 1?

4) Write O for odd and E for even underneath each of these numbers.

40	33	26	19	12	5
[ ]	[ ]	[ ]	[ ]	[ ]	[ ]

7	45	62	84	29	38
[ ]	[ ]	[ ]	[ ]	[ ]	[ ]

5) Fill in the missing numbers.

(+4)   13   [ ]   [ ]   [ ]   [ ]   33

(−3)   55   [ ]   [ ]   [ ]   [ ]   40

(−6)   36   [ ]   [ ]   [ ]   [ ]   6

Picture data

Pictograms and graphs are useful
ways to show information.

A farmer had 20 chickens. The pictogram shows
how many eggs he collected each day for a week.

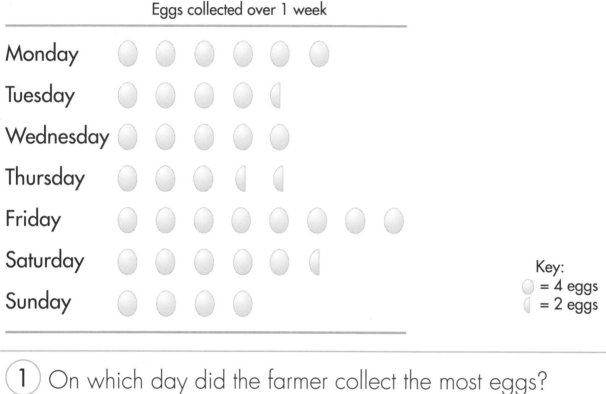

Eggs collected over 1 week

Key:
◯ = 4 eggs
◖ = 2 eggs

1) On which day did the farmer collect the most eggs?

....

2) How many eggs did the farmer collect on Tuesday?

3) How many more eggs did the farmer collect on
Saturday than Sunday?

Time filler:
Count how many jumps you and your
family or friends can do in two minutes.
Draw a pictogram to show the results.
What symbol will you use?

4 Look at the pictogram on page 32. Colour in the blocks
to show how many eggs the farmer collected each day.

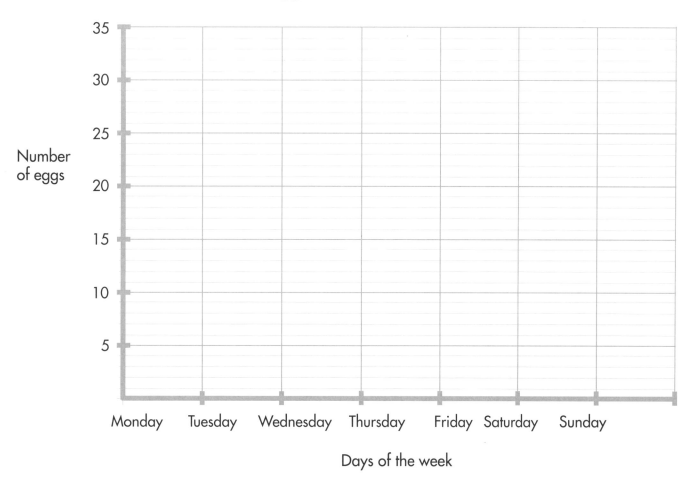

Eggs collected over one week

5 What is the total number of eggs collected on
Wednesday and Thursday?

Patterns

Look carefully to complete
these patterns. You will need
some colouring crayons.

(1) Complete the pattern.

(2) Fill in the missing shapes.

(3) Complete the arrow pattern.

Time filler:
Design your own patterns. Use shapes, colours, and sizes to vary your patterns.

(4) Complete the pattern on the necklace.

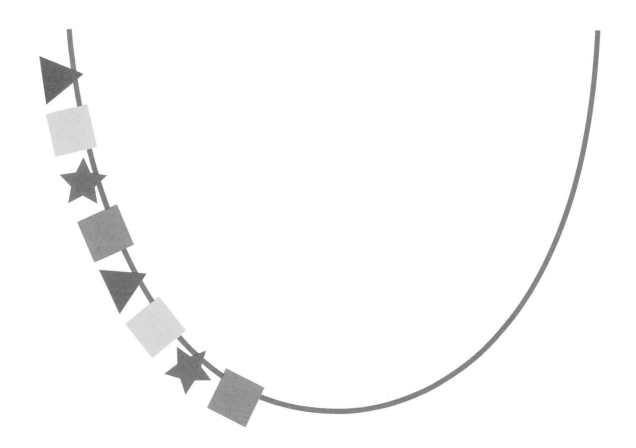

(5) Fill in the faces.

Rounding numbers

Rounding a number to the nearest ten is a useful way to make a quick estimate.

1. These numbers have units of 5 or more. Round them up to the next ten.

   36 rounds up to ☐

   49 rounds up to ☐

   25 rounds up to ☐

2. Circle the numbers with units less than 5.

   18   34   62   78   53

3. Round these numbers down. Remember to keep the tens digit the same.

   21 rounds down to ☐

   64 rounds down to ☐

   83 rounds down to ☐

Time filler:
Try estimating how many biscuits there are in a packet and how many sweets are in a bag.

4 There are 11 blue sweets, 24 yellow sweets, and 9 green sweets in a jar. Estimate to the nearest 10 how many sweets there are.

5 Link these numbers to the nearest 10. Draw lines.

27

12   10

36   20

42   30

17   40

23   50

48

Time facts

It is time to be alert and ready
to answer some questions all
about time. Start the timer.

(1) Match the time facts. Draw lines.

Hours in a day	12
Days of the week	10
Months of the year	52
Years in a decade	24
Weeks in a year	7

(2) Circle the clock that says 8.30.

(3) How many minutes are there in 1 hour?

Time filler:
What can you do in ten minutes?
Think of some activities such as the
number of pages of a book you can
read or the number of times you can
throw and catch a ball. Use the timer.

④ Show these times on the clocks.

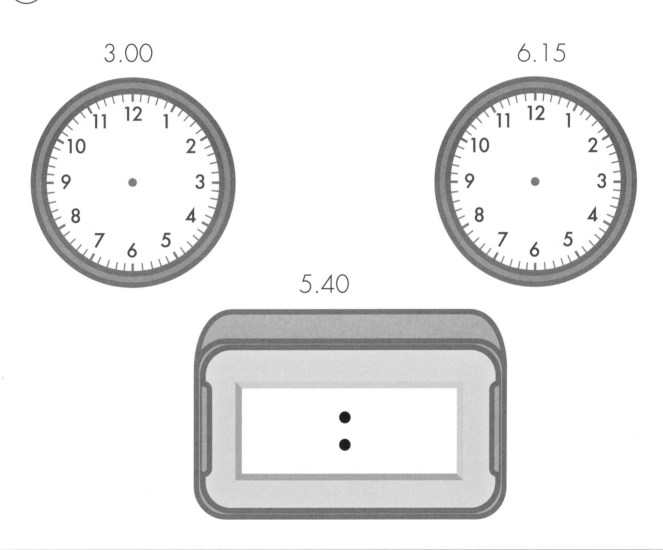

3.00

6.15

5.40

⑤ The station clock says 2.20. The train arrives at 2.30.
How long do the passengers have to wait?

Beat the clock 2

Can you finish all these adding
and subtracting sums in 10 minutes?
Ready, set, go!

(1) $2 + 7 =$

(2) $12 + 17 =$

(3) $22 + 27 =$

(4) $8 + 4 =$

(5) $18 + 24 =$

(6) $10 + 25 =$

(7) $32 + 15 =$

(8) $9 + 11 =$

(9) $19 + 41 =$

(10) $5 + 33 =$

(11) $9 - 4 =$

(12) $19 - 4 =$

(13) $29 - 14 =$

(14) $5 - 2 =$

(15) $45 - 12 =$

(16) $35 - 22 =$

(17) $64 - 33 =$

(18) $57 - 25 =$

(19) $27 - 15 =$

(20) $77 - 35 =$

(21) $66 + 14 =$

(22) $72 + 8 =$

(23) $21 + 19 =$

(24) $53 + 27 =$

(25) $48 + 12 =$

(26) $69 + 11 =$

(27) $24 + 56 =$

(28) $17 + 83 =$

(29) $30 + 70 =$

(30) $45 + 75 =$

Time filler:
Have you checked your answers? Then stop the timer. How long did it take you? Mark the answers. They are on page 80.

31) $8 - 5 =$

32) $28 - 15 =$

33) $58 - 35 =$

34) $7 - 2 =$

35) $57 - 22 =$

36) $87 - 42 =$

37) $6 - 5 =$

38) $36 - 15 =$

39) $96 - 25 =$

40) $56 - 45 =$

41) $7 + 4 =$

42) $57 + 64 =$

43) $5 + 9 =$

44) $45 + 29 =$

45) $6 + 8 =$

46) $76 + 18 =$

47) $9 + 9 =$

48) $49 + 39 =$

49) $7 + 8 =$

50) $47 + 18 =$

51) $13 - 7 =$

52) $33 - 17 =$

53) $15 - 8 =$

54) $55 - 28 =$

55) $14 - 6 =$

56) $84 - 46 =$

57) $11 - 4 =$

58) $31 - 24 =$

59) $71 - 44 =$

60) $100 - 95 =$

Multiplying numbers

Times, lots of, and groups of are all words that mean to multiply. These questions multiply by 2s, 5s, and 10s.

1. Mum has 2 baskets. 4 apples are in each basket. How many apples are there altogether?

2. What are 3 lots of 5?

3. Double these numbers.

3

5

7

Time filler:
Multiplying is a quick way of adding. Look at an analogue clock. Multiply each number by 5 and that will tell you how many minutes past an hour it is. Give it a go!

(4) Complete these questions.

3 x 10 =

8 x 10 =

5 x 5 =

2 x 2 =

(5) There were 4 flower pots. Each pot had 5 plants. How many plants were there altogether?

Measuring liquids

These questions are all about measuring liquids. Start the timer.

---

① Which holds the most liquid? Tick (✔) the answer.

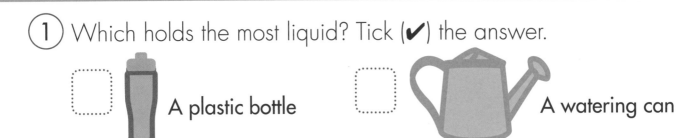

☐ A plastic bottle   ☐ A watering can

---

② What would you use to measure 200 ml of water? Circle the answer.

 A measuring tape    A measuring jug

---

③ Match the object with its volume. Draw a line.

 A bottle of water   2 litres

 A barrel of oil   300 millilitres

 A bottle of lemonade   160 litres

Time filler:
Fill some empty bottles of different sizes with water. Pour each one into a measuring jug to see how much water each bottle contained.

(4) How much water is in these jugs?

(5) Connor filled up a jug with 50 ml of orange juice and then added 200 ml of water.

How much liquid was in the jug altogether?

Dividing numbers

Knowing your 2, 5, and 10 times tables will help you work out these questions. Start the timer!

1) A pizza was cut into 8 slices. How many slices would 2 children each have?

2) What is 20 divided by 5?

3) Halve these numbers.

8   14   22

Time filler:
How many members are in your family? If you shared 20 sweets equally, how many would you each get? Are there any sweets left over?

(4) Complete these questions.

$40 \div 10 =$ [ ]

$70 \div 10 =$ [ ]

$35 \div 5 \; =$ [ ]

$16 \div 2 \; =$ [ ]

(5) A clown had 15 balloons to hand out equally to 5 children. How many balloons would each child get?

[ ]

Directions

These questions are all
about turns and position.
Are you sitting comfortably?
If yes, then press start.

1. Show where the arrow will point to if
   it makes a quarter turn anti-clockwise?

N

2. Mark the right angles on this
   house shape.

3. Which compass direction is opposite north?

....

Time filler:
Use a compass and explore your bedroom. What direction is your bed from the door – north, south, east, or west? What direction is your cupboard from the bed? Make a plan of your bedroom layout.

④ Draw a circle in D1.

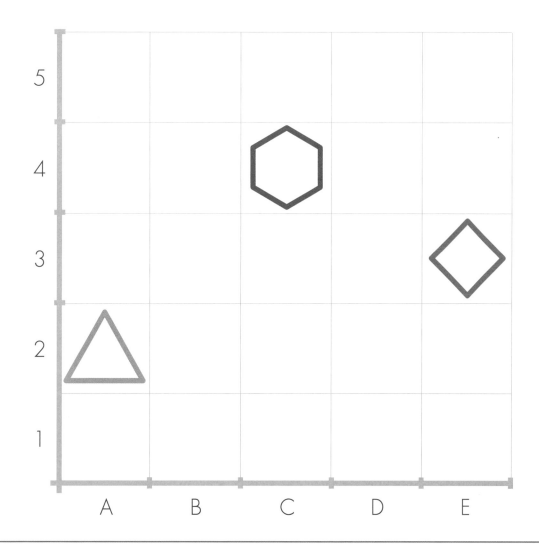

⑤ What position on the grid are these shapes?

Triangle ⬚   Diamond ⬚   Hexagon ⬚

Times tables

Do you know your 2s, 5s,
10s, 3s, and 4s times tables?
If so, then you are ready
to answer these questions.

① Move along the number line counting in groups of 3.

0 1 2 3 4 5 6 7 8 9 10 11 12 13 14 15 16 17 18 19 20 21 22 23 24 25 26 27 28 29 30

② Complete the number sentence.

If 8 x 3 = 24, then 3 x 8 = ☐

③ Circle the multiples of 4.

12   21   28   35   40

(4) Complete the multiplication square.

X	1	2	3	4	5
1		2		4	
2	2	4	6		10
3	3		9	12	
4	4	8	12		20
5		10		20	

(5) Fill in these steps.

5 x 2 = ☐   7 x 2 = ☐

10 x 2 = ☐   14 x 2 = ☐

5 x 4 = ☐   7 x 4 = ☐

Diagrams

Carroll diagrams and Venn diagrams
show how things are sorted into groups.

	Odd numbers	Even numbers
Less than 10	3	8
More than 10	21	14

① Add these numbers onto the diagram above.
   6   15   27   32

② In the diagram, which odd number is less
   than 10?

Time filler:
Draw the Venn diagram below onto another piece of paper and add some other animals and 4-legged objects. How many can you think of?

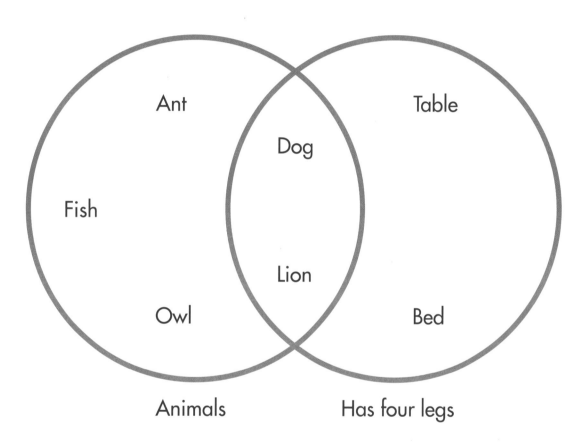

Ant

Table

Dog

Fish

Lion

Owl

Bed

Animals   Has four legs

3 On this diagram, which animals have four legs?

....

4 On this diagram, which animals do not have four legs?

....

5 Add a drawing of a chair onto the diagram.

Shopping

Getting to know all about using
money is very helpful especially
for when you go shopping.

1. Circle the three coins you would use
   to make 35p?

2. A pencil costs 5 pence. How much
   would 3 pencils cost?

3. A pen costs 12 pence. How much change
   will you get from 20 pence?

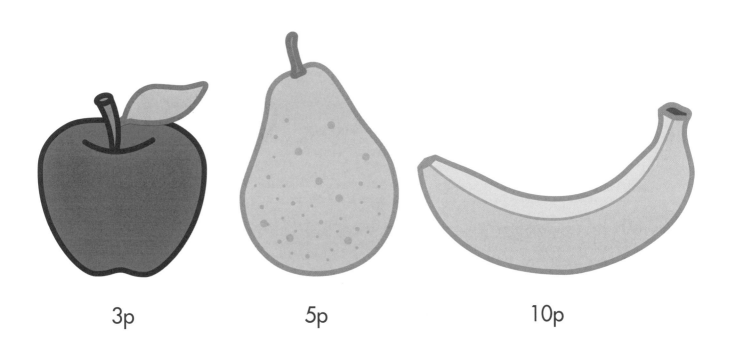

3p   5p   10p

(4) How much will 3 apples and 1 pear cost?

(5) A woman buys 7 bananas. How much change does she get from £1.00?

Measuring speed

Speed is measured in kilometres or miles per hour. How quickly will you zoom through these questions?

① Which is faster? Circle the answer.

A car

A bicycle

② What would you use to measure the speed of a runner? Circle the answer.

A stop watch

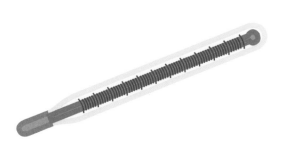

A thermometer

③ Match the object with its speed. Draw a line.

Racing car   70 miles/hr

Cheetah   4 miles/hr

A person walking   220 miles/hr

Time filler:
Write down your top ten favourite animals.
Put them in order of which ones you think will
be the fastest to slowest movers. Ask an adult
to help you find out the fastest speed of these
animals. Was your estimated order correct?

4. Look at these times on the stopwatches. Which was the
   fastest runner in a 1,000 metre race? ....

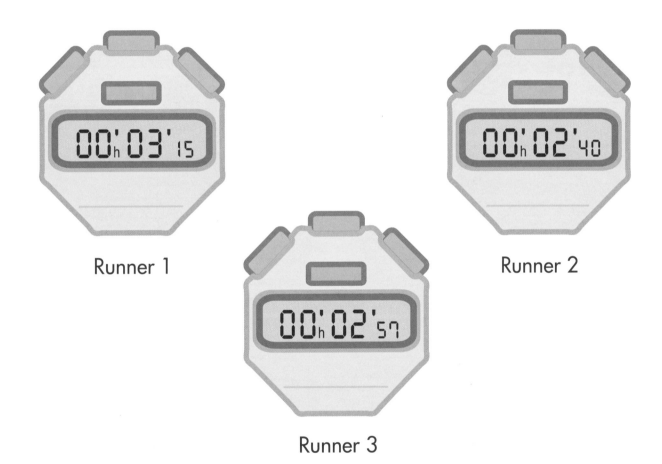

Runner 1   Runner 2

00ʰ03'15   00ʰ02'40

00ʰ02'57

Runner 3

5. A cyclist travelled at 25 kilometres per hour along the road.
   He cycled at 12 kilometres per hour up a hill. How much
   slower did he cycle when going up the hill?

Problem solving

Read these questions carefully and work out if they are asking you to add, subtract, multiply, or divide.

(1) There were 15 biscuits. Jared ate 6. How many were left?

....

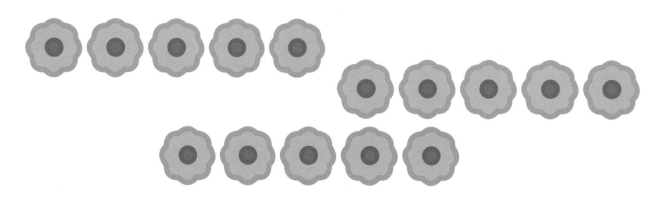

(2) Mum had 13 mugs. She was given a set of 6 mugs. How many mugs did she have altogether?

....

(3) There were 24 sweets in a jar. They were shared equally between 3 children. How many sweets did each child have?

....

(4) There were 5 bowls. There were 6 cherries in each bowl. How many cherries were there altogether?

....

(5) Ryan bought a pencil for 5 p, a notepad for 30 p, and an eraser for 12 p. How much change did he get from 50 pence?

....

More 3-D shapes

Here are some more questions about comparing 3-D shapes.

① Which is the net of a cube? Circle the answer.

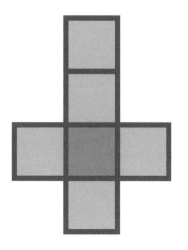 

② Circle the shape with the most faces.

 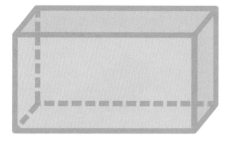

Triangular prism   Cuboid

③ Which shape has no edges? Circle the answer.

A sphere   A cylinder

Time filler:
Find some empty tubes, boxes, and other recycled packaging. What sort of sculpture can you make by sticking them together?

(4) Label these shapes and count the vertices (corners).

Name ....
Number of vertices ....

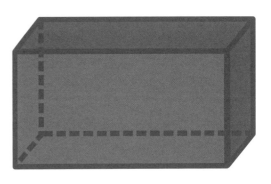

Name ....
Number of vertices ....

Name ....
Number of vertices ....

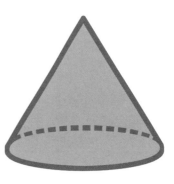

Name ....
Number of vertices ....

(5) Which shape has 5 faces, 5 vertices (corners), and 8 edges?

....

Fractions

A fraction is a part of a whole.
You will need some coloured
crayons to do these questions.

(1) Colour in ¼.

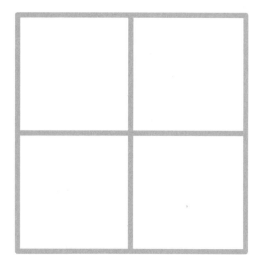

(2) Tick (✔) the shape that shows ⅓.

(3) How many halves are there in a whole one?

Time filler:
Draw around a circular plate on a piece of paper. Cut out the circle and then start folding it. Fold it in half, then quarters, then eighths, and then sixteenths. Between each fold, open up the circle and count the number of segments you have made.

4 Here are 8 butterflies. Colour in half of them.

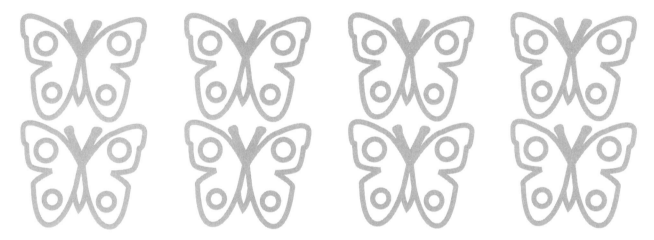

Fill in the answer: ½ of 8 = ⬚

5 Here are 12 balloons. Colour a quarter of them.

Fill in the answer: ¼ of 12 = ⬚

Beat the clock 3

Can you finish all these times
tables questions in 10 minutes?
Start the clock.

1) 2 x 2 =

2) 3 x 4 =

3) 4 x 3 =

4) 5 x 5 =

5) 6 x 2 =

6) 8 x 10 =

7) 9 x 2 =

8) 3 x 5 =

9) 2 x 7 =

10) 7 x 3 =

11) 20 ÷ 10 =

12) 12 ÷ 2 =

13) 9 ÷ 3 =

14) 8 ÷ 4 =

15) 50 ÷ 5 =

16) 22 ÷ 2 =

17) 16 ÷ 4 =

18) 16 ÷ 2 =

19) 3 ÷ 3 =

20) 8 ÷ 2 =

21) 4 x 2 =

22) 5 x 3 =

23) 7 x 1 =

24) 3 x 7 =

25) 1 x 11 =

26) 2 x 5 =

27) 5 x 4 =

28) 4 x 5 =

29) 6 x 3 =

30) 3 x 2 =

Time filler:
Have you checked your answers? Then stop the timer. How long did it take you? Mark the answers. They are on page 80.

(31) $10 \div 5 =$

(32) $14 \div 2 =$

(33) $40 \div 10 =$

(34) $25 \div 5 =$

(35) $4 \div 4 =$

(36) $30 \div 5 =$

(37) $60 \div 10 =$

(38) $6 \div 2 =$

(39) $15 \div 5 =$

(40) $12 \div 3 =$

(41) $5 \times 7 =$

(42) $8 \times 2 =$

(43) $9 \times 1 =$

(44) $10 \times 10 =$

(45) $4 \times 7 =$

(46) $6 \times 4 =$

(47) $4 \times 8 =$

(48) $3 \times 9 =$

(49) $10 \times 8 =$

(50) $3 \times 3 =$

(51) $18 \div 3 =$

(52) $50 \div 10 =$

(53) $40 \div 5 =$

(54) $18 \div 2 =$

(55) $30 \div 3 =$

(56) $24 \div 4 =$

(57) $45 \div 5 =$

(58) $24 \div 2 =$

(59) $110 \div 10 =$

(60) $36 \div 4 =$

Answers:

4–5 Place value
6–7 Measuring length

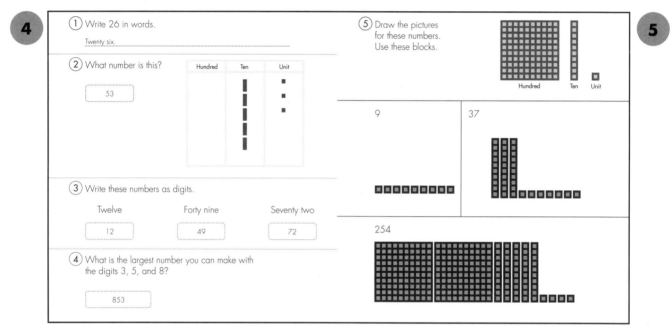

Working with hundreds, tens, and units is an important part of early mathematical understanding. Although the spellings of some of the numbers are complicated, they will be very useful for your child to know. See pages 20–21 for some further number words to practise.

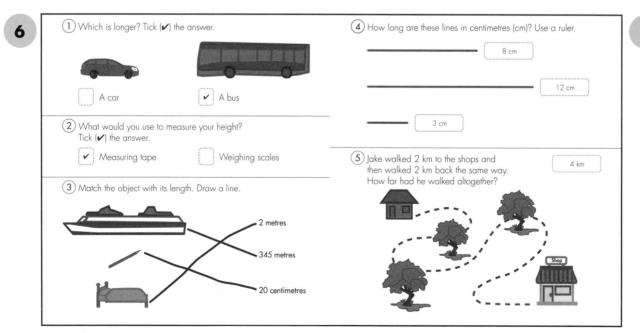

These pages encourage your child to become confident comparing and measuring lengths. At this stage, she/he is starting to be introduced to the units of measuring lengths, which can be confusing and daunting. When travelling, encourage your child to be aware of distances covered and begin to use the terminology.

Answers:

8–9 Counting
10–11 2-D shapes

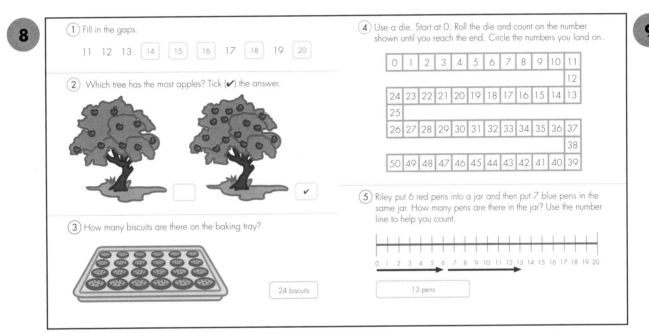

Encourage your child to count objects at least up to 50. A number line will also help her/him identify the relationship and order of numbers. Playing board games with numbers, for example Snakes and Ladders, are great for reinforcing counting practice.

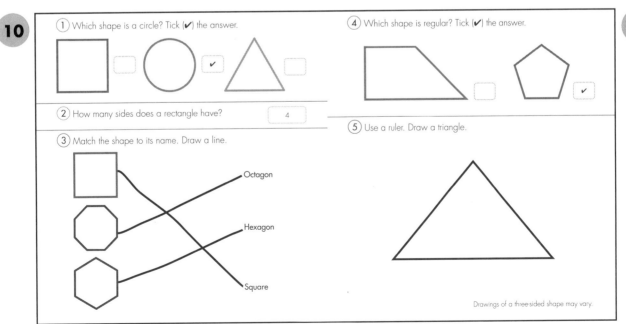

Knowing the names and properties of 2-D shapes will help your child recognize the differences between them. Also she/he will need to be on the lookout for whether a shape is regular or irregular. Talking about the shapes around them, for example food packaging, will help too.

Answers:

12–13 Counting in leaps
14–15 Tables and charts

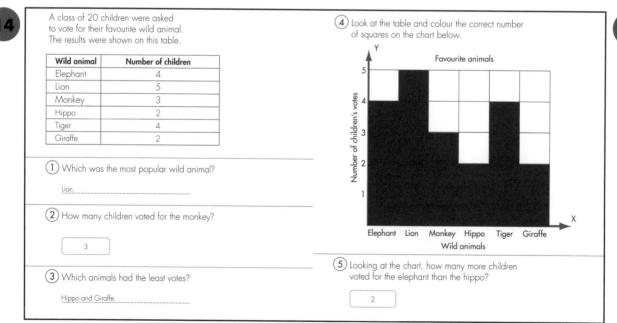

12

① Count in 2s. Fill in the gaps.

2 [4] 6 [8] 10 [12] [14] 16 [18] 20

② Here is a number line. Start at 7 and show the leaps to add 2 more each time.

7 8 9 10 11 12 13 14 15 16 17 18 19 20

③ Work out the missing numbers.

12 22 32 [42] [52] 62 [72]

5 10 [15] 20 [25] [30] 35 [40]

24 22 [20] 18 [16] 14 [12] 10

13

④ What is 5 more than 45?

[50]

⑤ This machine adds 10 to numbers. Add 10 to the numbers going IN and write the answers coming OUT.

IN
3 →
6 →
8 →
12 →
35 →

+10

OUT
[13]
[16]
[18]
[22]
[45]

When counting in 2s, children should realize that if they begin on an odd number they will continue on odd numbers, and vice versa with even numbers.

For counting in 10s, the units digits stay the same and only the tens digits go up.

14

A class of 20 children were asked to vote for their favourite wild animal. The results were shown on this table.

Wild animal	Number of children
Elephant	4
Lion	5
Monkey	3
Hippo	2
Tiger	4
Giraffe	2

① Which was the most popular wild animal?

Lion.

② How many children voted for the monkey?

[3]

③ Which animals had the least votes?

Hippo and Giraffe.

15

④ Look at the table and colour the correct number of squares on the chart below.

Favourite animals

Y
Number of children's votes
5
4
3
2
1

Elephant Lion Monkey Hippo Tiger Giraffe
Wild animals
X

⑤ Looking at the chart, how many more children voted for the elephant than the hippo?

[2]

Techniques for reading simple grids will help children with complex ones later. To create the chart on page

15 by colouring the correct number of squares, your child may like to use a different colour for each animal.

Answers:

16–17 Number order
18–19 Lines of symmetry

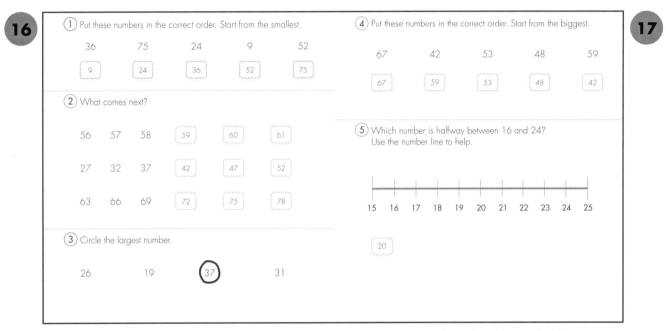

Arranging numbers in order helps to reinforce confidence in the value and concept of numbers. Check that your child is not reading and writing the numbers in reverse, such as 76 instead of 67. This indicates that they may need more practice on place value.

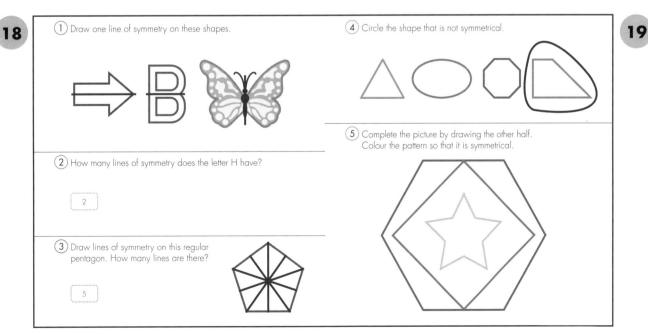

Is your child able to explain what a line of symmetry is? If they are finding this activity difficult, they could draw and cut out shapes on paper and fold them in half to see if they match and have any lines of symmetry. Putting a small mirror along the half-way line will also help to show how the other half will match.

Answers:

22–23 Adding numbers
24–25 Measuring weight

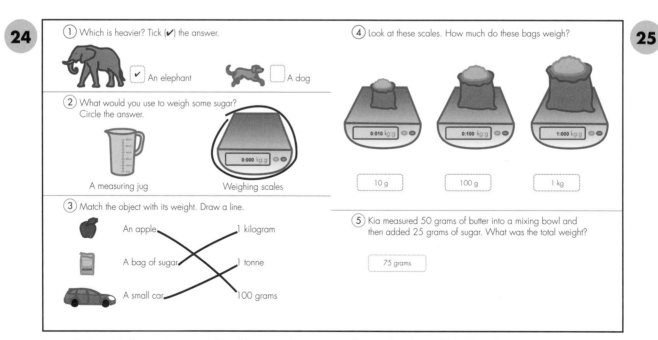

22

① What is the total of 5 and 8?

13

② Add together 12 and 16.

28

③ Fill out these steps:

40 + 20 = 60

8 + 6 = 14

48 + 26 = 74

23

④ Complete these sums:

28	34	52	47
+ 11	+ 25	+ 37	+ 19
39	59	89	66

⑤ 32 children went to school in one bus and 27 children in another bus. How many children were there altogether?

59

Encourage your child to look for ways to make the calculations easier. Knowing single-digit number bonds such as 5 + 6, 6 + 7, and 7 + 8 are very useful. If she/he is adding a number to the digit 9, it is easier to add 10 and then take away 1. These strategies will be useful for mental arithmetic skills too.

24

① Which is heavier? Tick (✔) the answer.

✔ An elephant   ☐ A dog

② What would you use to weigh some sugar? Circle the answer.

A measuring jug   Weighing scales
0:000 kg:g

③ Match the object with its weight. Draw a line.

An apple — 100 grams

A bag of sugar — 1 kilogram

A small car — 1 tonne

25

④ Look at these scales. How much do these bags weigh?

0:010 kg:g   0:100 kg:g   1:000 kg:g

10 g   100 g   1 kg

⑤ Kia measured 50 grams of butter into a mixing bowl and then added 25 grams of sugar. What was the total weight?

75 grams

Towards the end of Year 2, your child will begin to be introduced to units of measuring weight. Encourage your child to help you weigh out sugar, flour, or butter when cooking. Also if possible, allow them to measure the weight of fruits and vegetables for fun.

Answers:

26–27 Subtracting numbers
28–29 3-D shapes

26

① What is the difference between 18 and 5?

13

② Take away 26 from 58.

32

③ Fill out these steps.

30 – 28 = 2

64 – 30 = 34

64 – 28 = 36

27

④ Complete these questions.

25	38	55	47
– 13	– 24	– 37	– 19
12	14	18	28

⑤ Anya had a bag of 50 sweets. She gave 28 sweets to her friends. How many did she have left?

22

Let your child use a number line to help them calculate the answers if they need help visualizing the taking away. Encourage them to subtract the units first and then move on to the tens. There is space around the questions for the children to show their workings or set the problem out in a way that suits them.

28

① Which shape is a cube? Tick (✔) the answer.

✔

② How many faces does a square-based pyramid have?

5

③ Match the shape to its name. Draw a line.

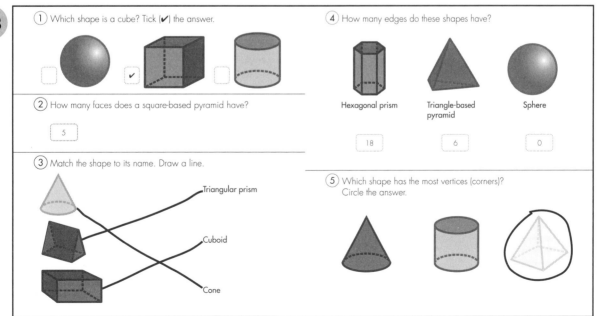

Triangular prism
Cuboid
Cone

29

④ How many edges do these shapes have?

Hexagonal prism — 18
Triangle-based pyramid — 6
Sphere — 0

⑤ Which shape has the most vertices (corners)? Circle the answer.

When discussing 3-D shapes, your child should start using mathematical language such as curved and flat faces, straight edges, and corners to describe and compare them. Encourage your child to find the shapes featured on the page at home so that she/he can feel the shape too.

72

Answers:

30–31 Sequences
32–33 Picture data

30

① Fill in the missing numbers.

6   10   14   [18]   22   [26]   [30]

23   30   37   [44]   [51]   58   [65]

② Circle the odd numbers in this sequence.

4   (7)   10   (13)   16   (19)

③ Fill in the missing numbers.

44   42   [40]   [38]   [36]   34   [32]

73   70   67   [64]   [61]   58   [55]

31

④ Write O for odd and E for even underneath each of these numbers.

40	33	26	19	12	5
E	O	E	O	E	O

7	45	62	84	29	38
O	O	E	E	O	E

⑤ Fill in the missing numbers.

(+4)   13   [17]   [21]   [25]   [29]   33

(−3)   55   [52]   [49]   [46]   [43]   40

(−6)   36   [30]   [24]   [18]   [12]   6

Your child needs to first look out for the rule that works through each sequence. Creating their own sequences will also help them to understand and look out for relationships between the order of numbers.

---

32 / **33**

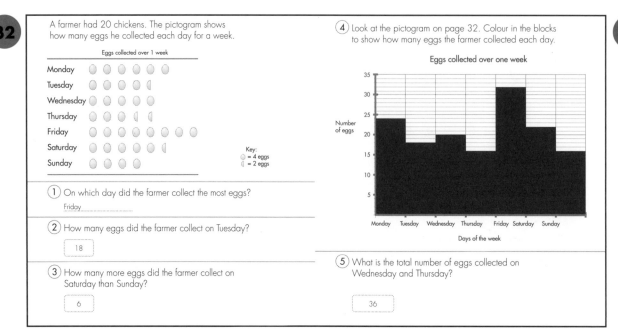

A farmer had 20 chickens. The pictogram shows how many eggs he collected each day for a week.

Eggs collected over 1 week

Key:
= 4 eggs
= 2 eggs

① On which day did the farmer collect the most eggs?

Friday

② How many eggs did the farmer collect on Tuesday?

18

③ How many more eggs did the farmer collect on Saturday than Sunday?

6

④ Look at the pictogram on page 32. Colour in the blocks to show how many eggs the farmer collected each day.

Eggs collected over one week

⑤ What is the total number of eggs collected on Wednesday and Thursday?

36

Pictograms are a fun visual way of presenting data. Make sure that your child notices the key, where one egg image represents four eggs and half an egg image represents two eggs. Encourage your child to work out the number of eggs collected for each day at the beginning.

Answers:

34–35 Patterns
36–37 Rounding numbers

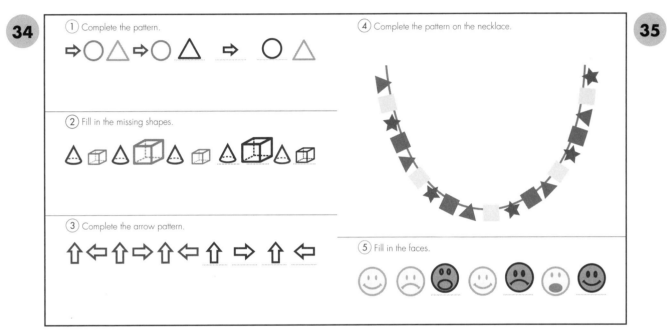

Spotting patterns made with different shapes, sizes, positions, and colours is a fun way of developing ordering skills. Encourage your child to describe the patterns she/he creates using mathematical language such as bigger, smaller, circles, squares, left or right arrow, up and down.

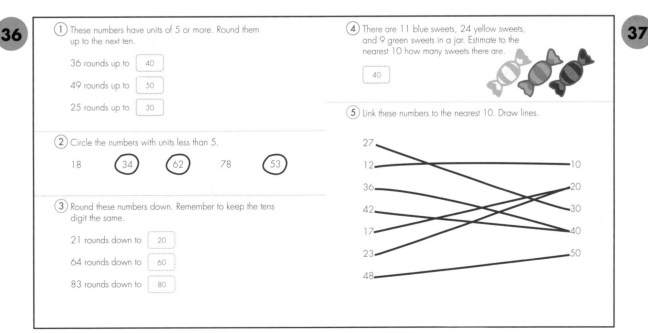

Remind your child to keep the tens the same if rounding down when the units are less than 5 and increase the tens if the units are 5 or more. Explain that rounding is a useful way of estimating answers. Your child could practise rounding when shopping to quickly estimate the total price of one or two things.

Answers:

38–39 Time facts
42–43 Multiplying numbers

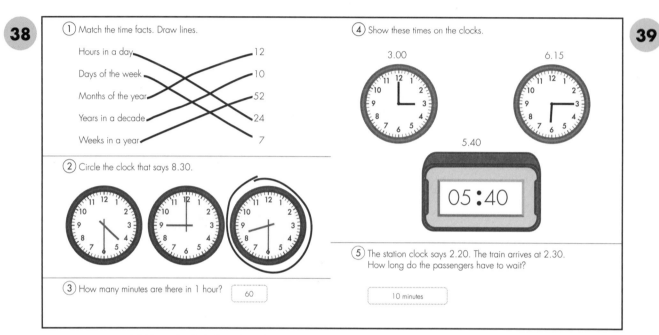

38

① Match the time facts. Draw lines.

Hours in a day — 24
Days of the week — 7
Months of the year — 12
Years in a decade — 10
Weeks in a year — 52

② Circle the clock that says 8.30.

③ How many minutes are there in 1 hour? 60

39

④ Show these times on the clocks.

3.00   6.15

5.40

05:40

⑤ The station clock says 2.20. The train arrives at 2.30. How long do the passengers have to wait?

10 minutes

Point out to your child how the little hour hand on an analogue clock moves on slowly. Its slightly changed position is important to show at the half past and quarter past. Encourage your child to practise saying the days of the week and months of the year in the correct order.

42

① Mum has 2 baskets. 4 apples are in each basket. How many apples are there altogether?

8

② What are 3 lots of 5?

15

③ Double these numbers.

3   5   7
6   10   14

43

④ Complete these questions.

$3 \times 10 =$ 30

$8 \times 10 =$ 80

$5 \times 5 =$ 25

$2 \times 2 =$ 4

⑤ There were 4 flower pots. Each pot had 5 plants. How many plants were there altogether?

20

Your child needs to be familiar with the 2x, 5x, and 10x tables before progressing with these pages. If your child needs to visualize the question, encourage her/him to draw sets such as 2 baskets with 4 apples in each, or 3 piles of 5 sweets for question 2.

Answers:

44–45 Measuring liquids
46–47 Dividing numbers

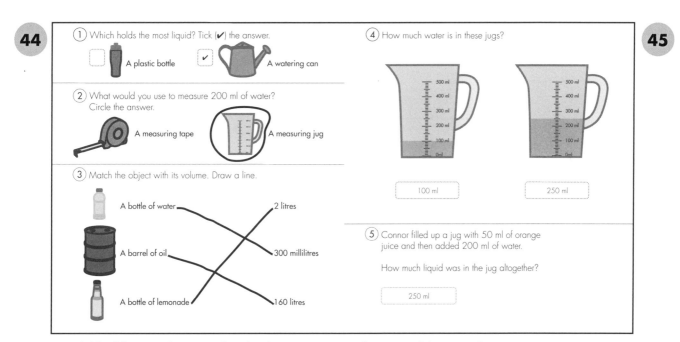

44

1) Which holds the most liquid? Tick (✔) the answer.

☐ A plastic bottle   ✔ A watering can

2) What would you use to measure 200 ml of water? Circle the answer.

A measuring tape   (A measuring jug)

3) Match the object with its volume. Draw a line.

A bottle of water ——→ 160 litres
A barrel of oil ——→ 2 litres
A bottle of lemonade ——→ 300 millilitres

45

4) How much water is in these jugs?

100 ml   250 ml

5) Connor filled up a jug with 50 ml of orange juice and then added 200 ml of water.

How much liquid was in the jug altogether?

250 ml

Your child will have just been introduced to the units of measuring liquids, such as millilitres and litres. Encourage your child to fill different-sized containers with water and then pour the amount into a measuring jug to see the amount or help you pour certain amounts of water, milk, or other liquids during cooking.

46

1) A pizza was cut into 8 slices. How many slices would 2 children each have?

4

2) What is 20 divided by 5?

4

3) Halve these numbers.

8   14   22
4   7   11

47

4) Complete these questions.

$40 \div 10 =$ 4

$70 \div 10 =$ 7

$35 \div 5 =$ 7

$16 \div 2 =$ 8

5) A clown had 15 balloons to hand out equally to 5 children. How many balloons would each child get?

3 balloons

Just like on pages 42–43, encourage your child to visualize the questions by drawing piles of sweets or coins and then distributing them out into the right number of groups in the space provided. Look out for opportunities which require sharing out an equal number, for example sharing sweets in a bag among the family.

Answers:

48–49 Directions
50–51 Times tables

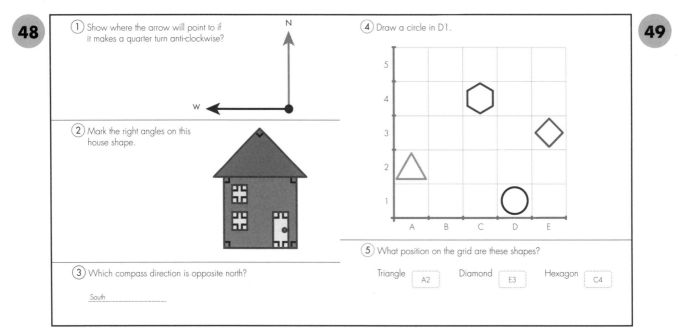

48

① Show where the arrow will point to if it makes a quarter turn anti-clockwise?

② Mark the right angles on this house shape.

③ Which compass direction is opposite north?

South

49

④ Draw a circle in D1.

⑤ What position on the grid are these shapes?

Triangle A2   Diamond E3   Hexagon C4

These questions are a mixture of challenges to encourage your child to think about position and turns. Show your child a compass and get out a few maps to show how the grid numbering works. Work out together the grid references of certain places and plan routes using directional language.

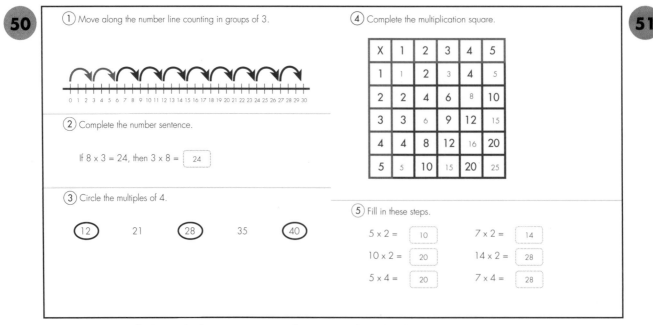

50

① Move along the number line counting in groups of 3.

② Complete the number sentence.

If 8 x 3 = 24, then 3 x 8 = 24

③ Circle the multiples of 4.

12   21   28   35   40

51

④ Complete the multiplication square.

X	1	2	3	4	5
1	1	2	3	4	5
2	2	4	6	8	10
3	3	6	9	12	15
4	4	8	12	16	20
5	5	10	15	20	25

⑤ Fill in these steps.

5 x 2 = 10   7 x 2 = 14

10 x 2 = 20   14 x 2 = 28

5 x 4 = 20   7 x 4 = 28

These pages cover further multiplication practice with 3x and 4x tables as well. Encourage your children to chant or sing the times tables they know to get the facts reinforced in their minds. Times table podcasts can be downloaded from the *www.dk.co.uk* website.

Answers:

52–53 Diagrams
54–55 Shopping

	Odd numbers	Even numbers
Less than 10	3	8 6
More than 10	21 15 27	14 32

(1) Add these numbers onto the diagram above.
6   15   27   32

(2) In the diagram, which odd number is less than 10?

3

Ant   Dog   Table   Fish   Lion   Owl   Bed

Animals   Has four legs

(3) On this diagram, which animals have four legs?

Dog, lion

(4) On this diagram, which animals do not have four legs?

Ant, fish, owl

(5) Add a drawing of a chair onto the diagram.

If your child needs some help, discuss with her/him what goes within each box on the Carroll diagram. For the Venn diagram, can your child explain why some of the words are in the overlapping section of the two circles?

(1) Circle the three coins you would use to make 35 p?

1p   2p   5p
10p   20p   50p

(2) A pencil costs 5 pence. How much would 3 pencils cost?

15 p

(3) A pen costs 12 pence. How much change will you get from 20 pence?

8 p

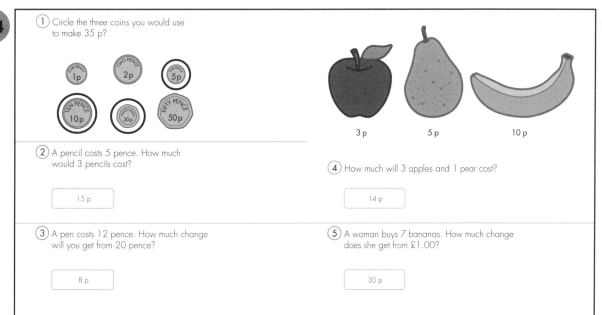

3 p   5 p   10 p

(4) How much will 3 apples and 1 pear cost?

14 p

(5) A woman buys 7 bananas. How much change does she get from £1.00?

30 p

Space has been provided for children to set out their workings or draw to visualize the problem. Remind them to write the unit (p or £) for each answer. There is no "p" needed if a "£" sign has already been used.

Answers:

56–57 Measuring speed
58–59 Problem solving

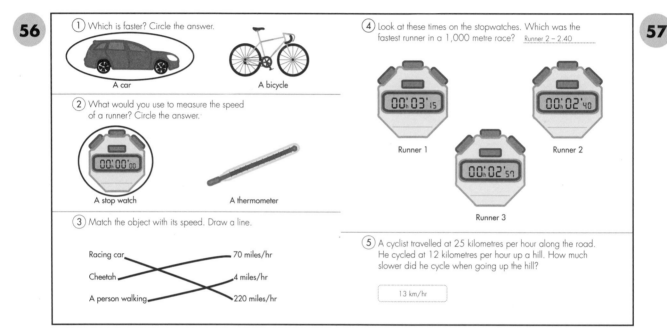

In the UK, children are introduced to both kilometres per hour and miles per hour as units of measuring speed. The questions challenge your child to think about comparing speeds, either based on their knowledge or looking at times on a stopwatch. If you have a stopwatch, do let your child use it to time themselves during an activity such as running from one point to another.

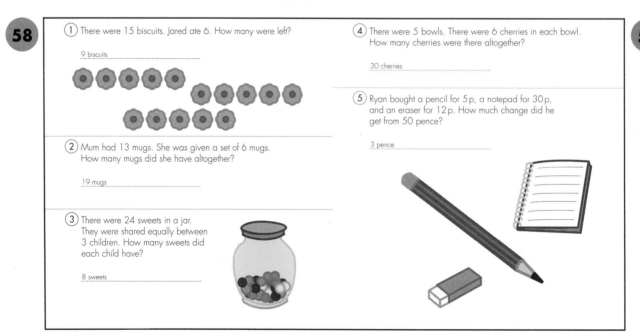

For problem solving, children will first have to decide what each question is asking them to do and then work out the best way to calculate the answer. For example, if they know their 5x table for question 4, it will be quicker to multiply rather than add 6 together five times.

Answers:

60–61 More 3-D shapes
62–63 Fractions

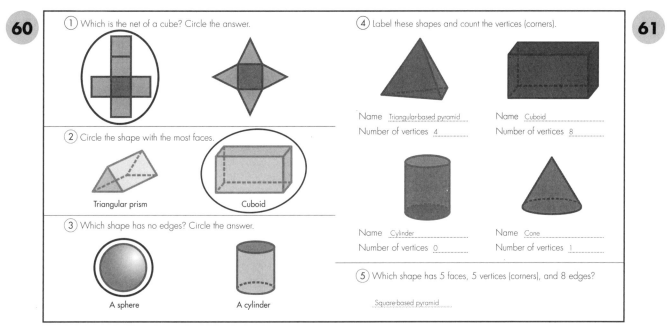

60 ① Which is the net of a cube? Circle the answer.

② Circle the shape with the most faces.

Triangular prism   Cuboid

③ Which shape has no edges? Circle the answer.

A sphere   A cylinder

61 ④ Label these shapes and count the vertices (corners).

Name Triangular-based pyramid
Number of vertices 4

Name Cuboid
Number of vertices 8

Name Cylinder
Number of vertices 0

Name Cone
Number of vertices 1

⑤ Which shape has 5 faces, 5 vertices (corners), and 8 edges?

Square-based pyramid

If your child is finding it difficult to count corners or identify faces from the diagrams, let them find real examples of the shapes in the kitchen, bathroom, or among their toys. Ask your child to talk about what makes these 3-D shapes different from each other.

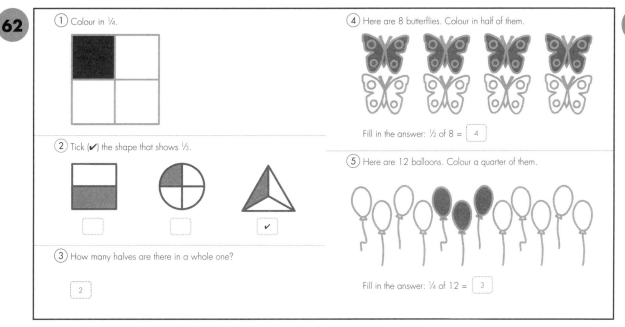

62 ① Colour in ¼.

② Tick (✔) the shape that shows ⅓.

③ How many halves are there in a whole one?

2

63 ④ Here are 8 butterflies. Colour in half of them.

Fill in the answer: ½ of 8 = 4

⑤ Here are 12 balloons. Colour a quarter of them.

Fill in the answer: ¼ of 12 = 3

For fractions of numbers and shapes, children should look at the bottom number of the fraction (denominator) to check how many groups the set or shape should be split into. For example, ¼ will need four equal parts.

To extend the activity, can your child work out how many balloons would be coloured in for two quarters and then three quarters?

Answers:

20–21 Beat the clock 1
40–41 Beat the clock 2
64–65 Beat the clock 3

You may wish to take a photocopy of these pages before your child begins so that she/he can do this exercise a number of times. Although this is against the clock, make sure that children do not feel pressurized to rush their answers. It is more important to be accurate as they could come back to try again and beat the clock at another time.

20 – 21

(1) 9	(2) 12	(3) 22		(31) 87	(32) 30	(33) 44
(4) 16	(5) 3	(6) 32		(34) 82	(35) 61	(36) 49
(7) 8	(8) 4	(9) 11		(37) 26	(38) 55	(39) 10
(10) 1	(11) 27	(12) 38		(40) 77	(41) 13	(42) 66
(13) 43	(14) 18	(15) 7		(43) 98	(44) 73	(45) 34
(16) 56	(17) 33	(18) 14		(46) 81	(47) 100	(48) 25
(19) 21	(20) 15	(21) 40		(49) 60	(50) 95	(51) 76
(22) 69	(23) 80	(24) 53		(52) 84	(53) 37	(54) 75
(25) 20	(26) 45	(27) 51		(55) 88	(56) 92	(57) 57
(28) 19	(29) 5	(30) 64		(58) 48	(59) 62	(60) 99

40 – 41

(1) 9	(2) 29	(3) 49		(31) 3	(32) 13	(33) 23
(4) 12	(5) 42	(6) 35		(34) 5	(35) 35	(36) 45
(7) 47	(8) 20	(9) 60		(37) 1	(38) 21	(39) 71
(10) 38	(11) 5	(12) 15		(40) 11	(41) 11	(42) 121
(13) 15	(14) 3	(15) 33		(43) 14	(44) 74	(45) 14
(16) 13	(17) 31	(18) 32		(46) 94	(47) 18	(48) 88
(19) 12	(20) 42	(21) 80		(49) 15	(50) 65	(51) 6
(22) 80	(23) 40	(24) 80		(52) 16	(53) 7	(54) 27
(25) 60	(26) 80	(27) 80		(55) 8	(56) 38	(57) 7
(28) 100	(29) 100	(30) 120		(58) 7	(59) 27	(60) 5

64 – 65

(1) 4	(2) 12	(3) 12		(31) 2	(32) 7	(33) 4
(4) 25	(5) 12	(6) 80		(34) 5	(35) 1	(36) 6
(7) 18	(8) 15	(9) 14		(37) 6	(38) 3	(39) 3
(10) 21	(11) 2	(12) 6		(40) 4	(41) 35	(42) 16
(13) 3	(14) 2	(15) 10		(43) 9	(44) 100	(45) 28
(16) 11	(17) 4	(18) 8		(46) 24	(47) 32	(48) 27
(19) 1	(20) 4	(21) 8		(49) 80	(50) 9	(51) 6
(22) 15	(23) 7	(24) 21		(52) 5	(53) 8	(54) 9
(25) 11	(26) 10	(27) 20		(55) 10	(56) 6	(57) 9
(28) 20	(29) 18	(30) 6		(58) 12	(59) 11	(60) 9